MW01599166

Life's Pathway in Poetry

Ralph Buelow

Halo
PUBLISHING
INTERNATIONAL

The views and opinions expressed in this book are those
of the author and do not necessarily reflect the official
policy or position of Halo Publishing International. Any
content provided by our authors are of their opinion and
are not intended to malign any religion, ethnic group, club,
organization, company, individual or anyone or anything.

ISBN: 978-1-63765-227-5
LCCN: 2022907113

Halo Publishing International, LLC
www.halopublishing.com

Printed and bound in the United States of America

This collection of poems is being dedicated to the entire Buelow family—my parents, Ralph and JoAnn; my lovely wife, Margarita; my four beautiful children; and my ten precious grandchildren. You have helped to create wonderful memories and life experiences for me. For this, I say thank you from the bottom of my heart.

Contents

Childhood 9

Adulthood 25

Career 64

Retirement 90

Recreation 103

Outdoors 124

Life Advice 135

Childhood

Baseball

I played a lot of baseball
As a young kid
I love America's past time
It's all I ever did

I tried out for little league
I had the wrong glove
I got myself a left-handed one
To play the game I love

I started in the outfield
Soon switched to first base
I batted third in the lineup
Known as the team's ace

I was voted annually
To play in the all-star game
The coaches and players
They all knew my name

We won the league championship
It was a lopsided win
I was perfect from the plate
Now the trophy ceremony begins

My last summer
I worked out with a pro
He told me I was a natural
Taught me hitting, how to throw

Taught me how to hit with power
How to throw a curve
I was a talented southpaw
Who had a lot of nerve

I was in a movie
I wore the Dodger blue
Kids were all around me
Memories sticking like glue

I stepped away over forty years
Retired then started to play
I am told I am a natural still
By the players to this day

This game of baseball
Keeps me youthful and strong
Being back on a baseball field
Is where I definitely belong

Brothers

Three brothers
Is what I had
Called the Buelow boys
Mom and Dad are glad

Four little boys
Giving Mom fits
When all cleaned up
We were hits

Laugh and play
Argue and fight
Mom would referee
With all her might

My parents worked
We had chores
Dishes and baking
Buffing hardwood floors

All close in age
But different in our ways
Life was simple
Those were the days

I loved sports
One loved to sing
One was handy
All did their own thing

My brothers had nicknames
And did not agree
I had no subtitle
Which was fine by me

At age eighteen
We all left home
Explore the world
Space to roam

Now we have families
Are all grown up
We are grown men
No longer just pups

We live miles apart
Love to disagree
We are still the Buelow boys
It's our family tree

Cartoons

Popeye the Sailor
Daffy Duck, Bugs Bunny
Cartoons for kids
All were funny

Foghorn Leghorn
Underdog and Mighty Mouse
Cartoons we watched
In our house

Tom and Jerry
Yosemite Sam and Elmer Fudd
Road Runner and Wile E. Coyote
None were duds

Rocky and Bullwinkle
Wally Gator, Yogi Bear
On Saturday morning
Television with a flare

On the scene
Arrives new cartoons
Kids love to watch
None too soon

Peppa Pig and Mighty Mike
Ninja Turtles, Paw Patrol
Kids still enjoying
Kids in control

Simpsons and South Park
Cartoons with a different twist
An older audience
Cartoons still exist

Animation and laughing
Great for all ages
Cartoons surviving
Through life's stages

Chores

What are chores
How hard can they be
Made by my parents
And done by me

Are they done on a farm
Milking the cows
Or gathering the eggs
Are you feeding the sows

Are they done in the house
Mopping the floors
Washing the dishes
I want these chores no more

Chores can be fun
Or made to bore
If not done right
You will need to do more

Chores will make you grow up
Not to be lazy
This thing called chores
Can drive you crazy

Driver's Education

Back in the day
When I went to school
Driver's ed was a class
It was pretty cool

Three areas of study
Simulator, class, and behind the wheel
Being able to drive a car
Was quite a big deal

No experience needed
Just a driver's permit
Teachers would instruct you
Wow, what a hit

Take all three classes
And pass them all
Three different teachers
No party or ball

At the end of the semester
And pass all three classes
Off to the courthouse
Oops, don't forget my glasses

I drive to school now
In my new used car
The students all stare at me
I feel like a star

Paperboy

They deliver twice a day
In the morning and afternoon
Papers have been dropped off
Delivery will begin soon

I grab my paper bag
I jump on my bike
My paper route is big
And quite a hike

Rain or snow
In the hot sun
When delivering my papers
I am having fun

Put them in the door
Under the mat
It's cold today
Better take my hat

Wednesday and Thursday
Is collection time
I need my changer
For quarters and dimes

On Saturday morning
I pay my bill
He comes to our house
It's no big thrill

Whatever is left
Is mine to keep
I made twenty dollars
Not bad for a week

I like my route
It brings me joy
In my neighborhood
I am the paperboy

Track

Track and field
Too many to choose
How will I pick
To win or lose

Do I want to run
Or do I jump
Thinking about track
Is getting me pumped

I need to train
And watch what I eat
I need to work out
So not to be beat

I think I will run
And use my legs
I will run long races
The coach hasn't begged

I will have to run miles
To learn not to tire
Running the two-mile
Will be my desire

The race is tough
Need to condition my mind
Learning how to breathe
Will keep me out of a bind

I line up to start
And listen for the gun
Learning how to pace
Is part of the run

I start the final lap
Picking up my speed
I want to win this race
That is my need

Waterskiing

I sit in the water
As the rope splits my skis
Handle held tight
My elbows at my knees

I yell, "Hit it"
The boat takes off fast
The rope becomes tight
Out of the water at last

I begin to stand up
And lean back on my skis
I start to lean out
Slightly bent at the knees

I weave left
Then I weave right
The waves are beating me
With all their might

I jump high in the air
And land on a wave
To ski on one ski
One must be brave

I throw quite a tail
As I zig back and forth
The water is my kingdom
The boat is my fort

Ralph Buelow • 23

I have conquered the river
With all its force
I know no boundaries
The waters are my course

The thrill of the speed
And the splashing of the skis
Brings me great satisfaction
And the thrills I need

Adulthood

Baby

Made from the love
Of husband and wife
After nine months
They start their new life

They enter this world
As pure as the snow
Our baby is crying
For that's all they know

We wrap them in a blanket
And hold our baby tight
In today's hard world
It will be a fight

We teach our baby
To crawl and walk
We teach or baby to eat
We teach our baby to talk

We teach our baby
Right from wrong
We teach our baby
To sing a song

We teach our baby
The ABC's
Our baby loves Mommy
Our baby loves me

We teach our baby to read
We teach them to write
We teach our baby love
We teach or baby not to fight

Our baby is growing
And it's time to start school
We teach our baby patience
Not to be stubborn like a mule

We emphasize family
We emphasize sharing
Our baby is loving
Our baby is caring

We hope our baby grows
With the morals we teach
We show are baby happiness
For this is what we preach

Best Friend

What is a friend
When did you meet
Was it during school
Or out in the street

Are you from the same state
Just what do you share
Do you like the same things
Do you both have hair

I met my best friend
While at work
No strange phenomena
Not even a quirk

Outside of work
We meet at the pub
We drink a bottle of wine
We eat some grub

We talk about politics
We talk about life
We share some headaches
And mention the wife

We have a few laughs
Talk about current news
We both agree in life
That we have paid our dues

When we are done
And try paying the bill
We argue whose turn
And have quite a thrill

When it's time to go home
We walk to the car
Give each other a hug
And wave bye to the bar

My best friend
Was a wonderful find
He understands my problems
Can help me out of a bind

I don't know what I would do
Without my best friend
We are like brothers
And will enjoy life to the end

Christmas Presents

The tree is all decorated
As presents line the floor
I wrote a letter to Santa
Asking him for no more

The stockings are hanging
The magical elf has been busy
Christmas anticipation
Is making me dizzy

Our son is excited
And can't wait for the day
The calendar is marked
Open presents and play

Paper is torn
And thrown every which way
I will be picking up paper
For the rest of the day

Laughing and giggling
Is part of the story
Pictures and memories
Will bring back the glory

Dad

Who is this man
How did he come to be
He married my mother
And helped to create me

They come in all sizes
Shapes and forms
Who is Dad
What is the norm

My dad works hard
Providing for Mom and me
Dad reads me stories
Bouncing me on his knee

My dad teaches me
Right from wrong
My dad teaches me
How to be strong

My dad is the rock
And that is the scoop
He helps my mother
By cleaning my poop

Dad mows the yard
And shovels the snow
Dad waxes the car
To give it a glow

Dad is there
When I need him the most
Dad gets me through life
To Dad I toast

As I grow up
A true model for me
Dad has a heart
As big as the sea

Family

It begins with two
The day you wed
You set your size
You make your bed

The same religion
Ethnically twined
The same sex
Who's to mind

Do we stay as two
Do we increase in size
Babies are priceless
Always surprised

Love and compromise
Willing to bend
Families will break
How do we mend

Love is questioned
Patience gets tested
Stay evenly tempered
Family has nested

Divorce is devasting
Separation is tough
Communication is vital
Spouses, enough guff

Children are precious
Used as pawns
Parents fighting
Family is gone

Anniversaries are special
Year after year
Commitment is crucial
Okay to cheer

Stay the course
Remember your vows
Family is worth it
Family is wow

First Home

Start with the bank
Get preapproved
Let's talk loans
Get in the groove

Bring proof of income
Last year's taxes
Feeling nervous
No one relaxes

Need a down payment
How much can you spend
Not willing to break
But willing to bend

Need a realtor
Been preapproved
Show me some houses
Get me in the mood

I want a condo
With a lanai
Fitness room also
Free Wi-Fi

I need a space
For washer and dryer
A pool is optional
Price getting higher

One or two bedrooms
With ceiling fans
Need energy efficient
That is the plan

Tile or hardwood
Great for floors
I hope my lanai
Has sliding glass doors

I don't need fancy
Nor brand-new
I hope my realtor
Has a clue

Close to work
Close to my son
A safe community
Not costing a ton

Grandchildren

They come in all sizes
Short and tall
Skinny and big
And we love them all

They come into the world
For grandparents to spoil
We laugh and play with them
While Mom and Dad toil

As a baby
We want to love and hold
Parents tell us to share
Now warned and told

We watch you crawl
And learn to talk
We watch you grow
And learn to walk

You excel through life
Year after year
Grandparents are proud
You tackle life without any fears

You are now a teenager
You begin to explore
You will make some mistakes
But grandparents still adore

Ralph Buelow • 37

Now you are an adult
Life is streaming fast
Grandparents will warn
Live and make life last

You now have your own family
Grandparents aging even more
No one can live forever
Love, laugh, live, not mourn

Guys' Day

A personal holiday
A day of no school
Just two guys hanging out
Two guys trying to be cool

Today I play softball
My son loves watching me play
Recognized by all the players
Known as the batboy, so they say

No game today, on to mini golf
Lunch at Chick-fil-A
A chocolate shake to drink
Need to get home to play

Arrive back home
Now tablet and video games
Loves to play Xbox and Wii
Who's to blame

Do a little schoolwork
Math and read
Work on typing skills
How many minutes he pleads

Time for some music
Need to cook dinner
Would like salmon or steak
My son is no beginner

Clear the dishes
Go take a walk
Cruise on his skateboard
Now I can't talk

Time for more games
Break for a snack
My son beats me soundly
My son has the knack

A day of pure fun
We play and play
This unique personal holiday
Known as Guys' Day

Life's Circle

Start from a cell
Grow and divide
Male or female
God will decide

Hugs and kisses
Diapers and messes
Boys in blue sleepers
Girls in pink dresses

We hold and we love
They play and they cry
We come to their rescue
Without ever asking why

As they grow and mature
And run off to school
Relationships are made
Life can be cruel

They graduate and marry
In the wink of an eye
Life has just changed
Without saying goodbye

And now they have kids
Life seems so much older
They start new jobs
And dare life to be bolder

Successes and failures
Are part of the game
You want your children
To seek fortune and fame

While enjoying their families
Parents grow old
Hearts are filled with love
Children doing what they are told

Life happens way too fast
Stop and smell the roses
And make life last

Make beautiful memories
And heavenly dreams
Life just passed you by
So it seems

I want it back
You cry and you scream
You pray for God's help
That all is just a dream

Live in the moment
And take nothing for granted
Bloom like a flower
And stay firmly planted

Life's Struggles

I have a new job
A degree from school
We bought our first home
With a huge swimming pool

I work long hours
And work very hard
The wife stays at home
And the kid plays in the yard

Day after day
And year after year
Things have to change
It's been made perfectly clear

Ten years have passed
And now we're apart
The love we once shared
It's still in my heart

I live by myself now
Just me and the walls
I am now judged by others
As having no balls

The day has come
And I can't wake up
No morning walk
Or coffee in my cup

I dwell in heaven
It's my new home
Words can't describe
The clouds I roam

I answer to God
And pray for His mercy
He cleanses my soul
Wearing my Packers jersey

I watch over you now
And visit quite often
My body is motionless
As it lies in a coffin

Close your eyes
You will envision me
Our son is smiling
And sitting on my knee

Marriage

We promise to love
We promise to cherish
We promise to honor
And our marriage not to perish

She wore a white gown
With flowers in her hair
The side of the dress split
For her leg to bare

We did not marry traditionally
We did it with flair
We rented a helicopter
And married in the air

We kiss at night
When we go to bed
Love fills my heart
Dreams fill my head

We both worked hard
To start our new life
We had a nice home
For me and my wife

We started in the Midwest
And soon moved South
My wife was upset
My foot in my mouth

Life got better
As the days went by
She gave birth to our son
I had tears in my eyes

We were a family
Filled with love
Our future was bright
Like the stars above

I remember that day
How it was so grand
Through hell and high waters
Our marriage must stand

Military Son

They graduate from high school
Go off and enlist
Want to defend our country
I get the gist

They are young men
Going off to war
Witnessing bombing and killing
What terrible horrors

They go off to boot camp
To become mentally strong
They need to prove
That they do belong

They graduate from boot camp
Receive their orders
Off to foreign countries
Inside terrorist borders

They are physically strong
Ready to fight
This foreign enemy
Is no delight

They are assigned a company
Then into battalions
Their courage will be tested
Much like a stallion's

He was on night patrol
Almost back to the base
Their Hummer exploded
A bomb had been placed

The explosion had killed
The soldiers on each side
My son in the middle
Had nowhere to hide

I received a phone call from Germany
In the middle of the night
This was no dream
But a nightmare with fright

He had a bad injury
Trauma to the head
I thought for a moment
My son was dead

He survived his injury
Received a Purple Heart
Two tours of duty
Army and son now depart

He now wears tattoos
His fingers have numbers
What do they stand for
One certainly wonders

My son still has bad dreams
Remembering that night
War leaves terrible scars
A soldier still fights

I am proud of my son
For what he has done
I love this soldier
My military son

Mom

Where do you start
What do you say
Mom is much needed
And receives no pay

She begins before birth
Taking care of her baby
Picks out a name
Telling Dad, no maybes

Mom kicks into full gear
When the baby is born
Working day and night
And totally worn

Mom takes care of the home
And nourishes her child
Mom still cooks meals
Mom is running wild

Baby begins to grow
Mom teaches baby to talk
Mom is still changing diapers
As baby begins to walk

No days off
No overtime pay
Just one fringe benefit
Watching baby play

Years go by
Children begin school
Mom can relax
Next to the pool

But Mom still worries
School can be tough
Children will be tested
Decisions are rough

Mom will be proud
When school is done
Now off to college
This battle won

My mom is a hero
Gentle as a dove
Mom's heart is genuine
And will always show love

My Birthday

One day of the year
That's all about you
A personal holiday
With tons to do

Birthday presents to open
Cards to read
Cake to bake
Chocolate, I plead

A party to plan
Invitations were sent
Where are my balloons
I scream and vent

My friends have arrived
The party begins
We need to play games
I hope I win

Time for cake
Scoop some ice cream
Where are my presents
Didn't mean to scream

I blow out my candles
After making a wish
Pass out the cake
I want a big dish

My friends gather round
I rip open my gifts
Paper is flying
Time is moving swift

The party is over
Another year gone by
The day has ended
A tear in my eye

My Daughter

The apple didn't
Fall far from the tree
My oldest daughter
Is the spitting image of me

Her nickname is Sunshine
Pretty long blonde hair
Loved dressing like Mommy
Couldn't help but stare

Her favorite expression
Making reservations for dinner
Going to be a doctor
Going to be a winner

Gifted as a child
Played in the band
Played high school softball
A great helping hand

An overachiever
All through school
Valedictorian of her class
Knowledge is her rule

Scholarships came in
From schools all around
Married her high school sweetheart
Staying homeward bound

Went on to college
Received her degree
Family life for my daughter
Definitely agrees

Now an entrepreneur
Raising four kids
Mom of the year
She has my bid

A creative mind
Thinks outside the box
Has a fantastic business
Cunning as a fox

A model in her town
A model at home
No time for herself
Needs helping gnomes

An angel from heaven
A generous heart
A true blessing for me
And extremely smart

She never gives up
Striving for brilliance
Her mind is amazing
Her body resilient

Runny Nose

Red and stuffed
My nose I blow
Hand me a Kleenex
It's starting to flow

I will breathe some herbs
Drink hot tea
My nose is still clogged
How can this be

I try some medicine
To keep out of my chest
Try to take a nap
My body needs rest

I try some Sudafed
To relieve my congestion
Loss of appetite
Less for digestion

Rub Vicks on my chest
So I can sleep
I toss and turn
Blanket in a heap

I awake in the morning
I breathe really deep
My nose stopped running
Oh, what a relief

Shaving

Electric razor
Straight razor and cream
The choice is yours
So it seems

Electric needs charging
And pre-shave lotion
Stands up the whiskers
All in one motion

Straight razor and cream
Used in the old days
Razors are sharp
Not for play

Used by barbers
In the Old West
Still used today
This shave is the best

Lather you face
Lather your head
Shaving is smooth
Sliding like a sled

If an overachiever
Shave legs and chest
Removes unwanted hair
No furry nest

Ladies shave too
Legs and armpits
Lather up good
Shave bit by bit

A lot of brand names
Too many to choose
Try one at a time
Nothing to lose

Stingray Bike

My first bike
Was made by Dad
A Stingray constructed
I was glad

Stingrays have a
Banana seat
Special handlebars
This bike looks neat

A special back tire
Could be slick
Rubber was laid
Know the trick

Great for wheelies
Riding on one tire
Pull the front up
Kids would admire

Made with gears
Up to three speeds
Hand disc brakes
If feel the need

Vacation

Where do we go
What do we see
Do we go to the mountains
Or visit the sea

Do we travel by plane
Do we go in the car
Some of our choices
Are way too far

Do we go north
To see some sights
Or do we go south
And take a flight

Do we go west
Where it's hot and dry
Let's try the east
Pack and goodbye

I think we will drive
It will be a long trip
Better make some coffee
I will need something to sip

We travel as family
Laugh and have fun
Driving in the summertime
While soaking up the sun

Vacation is relaxing
It's right and just
Family and memories
Make vacations a must

Valentine's Day

A day for love
A day for caring
The whole world knows
Time for sharing

As young kids
While in school
Valentines for all
A valentine fool

As we mature
The one we admire
We truly love
Our heart's desire

This day is special
We seek a gift
That shows our love
Their heart will lift

We buy them diamonds
We buy them flowers
Boxes of chocolates
Love is the power

A special evening
Time for romance
Dinner and wine
A little dance

We hold their hand
Say, "I love you"
Love is the bond
Love is the glue

Career

Budget

It's a six-letter word
Yet it's so cruel
It's the way of business
And that is the rule

Budget is an outline
Budget is a plan
Budget is the way
A business deals your hand

A budget determines purchases
A budget determines growth
A budget seals the deal
And you swear by that oath

A budget brings promise
A budget can bring jobs
A budget that is not made
Will make you sob

But if you make your budget
Or even exceed the goal
That budget is no longer valid
As you have broken that mold

Food Service

Not meant for everyone
Overworked and underpaid
Appreciated by the public
Advertising handmade

Look at the server
Learning the steps of service
Taking your order
Some guests making them nervous

Next is the grill cook
Cooking to order
Some are American
Some south of the border

The poor little busboy
Clearing the tables
Keep your tub on the chair
Make sure it is stable

The underappreciated dishwasher
Sweaty and wet
The backbone of staff
Clean dishes are set

Last is the cashier
They take your money
"Was everything good"
"Come back soon, honey"

Now we have the manager
Shirt and tie
Visiting the tables
Smiling, saying hi

Moving

The wife is upset
The kids are mad
My big promotion
Now has me sad

I want to promote
Live and explore
I'll tell you one thing
Moving is no easy chore

I need to sell the house
Or terminate my lease
Either way I go
It's hard to release

Started my new job
Told again it's time to move
I was just settling in
Getting my groove

I asked the boss why
He said, "You're the best I got"
Put a gun to my head
And squeeze the shot

I said OMG
You have to be kidding
Why isn't this job
Up for bidding

I need to go home
And deliver the news
I'm feeling sick
I'm feeling the blues

Moving is tough
And comes with a price
Prestige and money
Are really bad advice

Robbed

Leaving from work
Late one night
I was met by robbers
Not much to my delight

They came from behind
Put a gun to my head
I heard the trigger pull back
Now cooperate or be dead

I bypassed the alarm
Back inside the door
One hurdle down
No bodies on the floor

They saw my cleaning man
He began to stutter
Pistol-whipped his face
"Office this way," I muttered

Inside the office
I opened the safe
They took the money
Now feel very unsafe

I am gagged and hog-tied
Got away in my car
I have no injuries
But my memory is scarred

After a couple of hours
I got myself released
Found my cleaning man
Time to call the police

The police arrived
I filled them in
Questions and searching
Ah, the fun begins

I am finally back home
Telling my wife
Said I was robbed
Lucky to have my life

Given the next day off
To look at mug shots
Brought in a sketch artist
But no picture they got

Police found my car
Inside had been trashed
A lot to process
A lot to hash

I now keep my car
Close to the front door
My employees leave in pairs
No more closing horrors

I look back now
Ask myself how I survived
My guardian angel was with me
I am lucky to be alive

Security Guard

A class D license
Is what you need
Forty hours of class
You have done your deed

Record and observe
Is our motto
The security gate
Is the grotto

Uniform is clean
Uniform is pressed
Need to look sharp
Need to impress

Watching the cameras
To protect the residents
Community is proud
You feel like the president

Shifts can be long
Shifts can be split
Your relief doesn't show up
Just moan a bit

I'm on patrol
You're at the gate
Conflict can happen
There is no hate

A visitor arrives
That wasn't called in
The guard says no
The fun begins

You deny them access
Suggest they call
The resident is upset
Now behind the eight ball

It comes with the territory
But follow the rules
One may say
Stubborn as a mule

When I go home
The shift is complete
Climb into bed
Get plenty of sleep

The Actor

When I was eighteen
I received a call
They needed a fill-in actor
One who plays baseball

A movie of a man
From prison to ball
A youth in Detroit
Was his fall

Career started in Iowa
Then on to Detroit
A prison inmate
They tried to exploit

No lines to rehearse
I was able to ad-lib
When opportunity arose
My lines I did

I met the actor
Who portrayed Ron LeFlore
His name was LeVar Burton
I simply adored

We sat and we talked
Played some ball
I was an actor
No time to fall

I played an LA Dodger
Wearing this uniform
Got kids excited
Which is the norm

Wearing the Dodger blue
Raised some commotion
Boys love baseball
Shows in their emotion

The movie itself
Made memories to relive
People can make mistakes
Society needs to forgive

The Job

A job is work
That must be done
It can weigh on your mind
And feel like a ton

It can be washing the dishes
Or mowing the grass
Jobs are commitments
You need to outlast

As you get older
You begin to get paid
Go to the bank
Save the money you made

Do I go on to college
And follow the norm
Live with Mom and Dad
Life's simplest form

Do you use your degree
To start your career
Absorbed by the workplace
Shift into high gear

A job pays the bills
Puts a roof over your head
Listening to one's boss
Will get you ahead

Bosses are great
Some you will spite
Change your career
The tunnel has light

The job is tough
Pick something you like
Life is a journey
A very long hike

Jobs can be nine to five
Some are twenty-four seven
Make a wrong choice
Now dead in heaven

Find the job
That you can enjoy
Working in a corporation
Or being self-employed

The Manager

I sit at my desk
And email I read
I ponder the question
How do I lead?

You clap and you cheer
You lead from the front
Some will be motivated
Others will grunt

I will grow and develop
We will read and train
This is way too much material
It scrambles my brain

You are doing a great job
You need to improve
You will lose your job
Better find your groove

I write evals
And hand out raises
I work long, hard hours
Without any praises

They scream, "P and L"
And "Make us lots of money"
I go home at night
And complain to my honey

The pressure is mounting
It's beginning to matter
Climb to success
Or fall off the ladder

I look in the mirror
And ask is all a loss?
I suck in my gut
And say, "No, I am the boss"

Trains

The earliest trains
Were powered by steam
Today, most eco-friendly way to travel
So it seems

Next generation of trains
Were powered by coal
Wagons and cars
Is what they pulled

Finally comes diesel
Pulling 40 percent of world's freight cargo
The number keeps growing
Maybe to Key Largo?

The East and West
Was finally united
Still pulling freight
Passengers excited

My grandpa was an engineer
Running Clinton to Boone
Dad would go with Grandpa
Departing before noon

Interview

What do you say
What do you ask
An important tool
An important task

Are you properly prepared
Are you properly trained
Ask specific questions
Need to pick their brain

Please, no yes-or-no questions
Do not ask their age
Be a great listener
You set the stage

You may ask to record
To play back later
Be positive, take notes
We are not debaters

Notice if they are punctual
Do they sit up straight
These are valuable indicators
To be great out of the gate

Ask the same questions
In more than one way
Do they give similar responses
Or do they really sway

Is eye contact made
Or are they looking down
One should answer with a smile
Instead of wearing a frown

Did they do their homework
Know history of your firm
Are they answering confidently
Or do they squirm

When the interview is complete
Know what makes them tick
You want to hire successfully
You want an employee to stick

Half Marathon: I competed in several half marathons, always fin-
ishing in the top ten percent of the field. This last half marathon,
I finished in the top one percent of the field at age fifty-four.

Dad: Age ninety-three and the
inspiration for my poem "Dad."
My father has been my mentor
and rock.

Mom: Age eighty-eight and the inspiration for my poem "Mom." My mother has a heart of gold and is a very generous and loving individual.

Military Son: My oldest son did two tours—Iraq and Afghanistan. My son is still fighting to protect Americans; he works in a hospital.

The Actor: At age nineteen, I was fortunate to be asked to play a Los Angeles Dodger baseball player in this movie starring LeVar Burton. I was able to talk with him one-on-one.

Guys' Day: My youngest son loves it when there is no school and he and I spend the day together. Always lunch at Chick-fil-A.

My Birthday: This is a picture of my youngest at his tenth birthday party. He brings a lot of joy to my life.

Senior Softball: My favorite pastime. I am in a senior softball league that runs November to April. Makes me feel very youthful again.

Christmas Cookies: My youngest son baking Christmas cookies using my grandmother's recipes. Tradition and holidays really go well together and are great for a family.

Grandchildren: Seven of my ten grandchildren.
I love and miss them. Wish I could see them more often.

Grandchild: My youngest grand-
child lives on the other side of
the United States. I truly miss
her; she's a sweetheart.

Marriage: My wife's dream was to marry in a helicopter, so
I made it a reality. Her parents, my oldest brother, the minister,
and I took to the skies, hovered over our apartment at that time,
and said our vows. What a wonderful way to be married.

My Daughter: My oldest daughter, who is quite the entrepreneur, thinks well outside the box. She has a beautiful family and is also on the city council.

Best Friend: My best friend is my former boss. We are both from the state of Iowa. We meet twice a month at the local pub. Great discussions and laughter.

Retirement

Cruise

How long of a trip
Where to cruise
Better tell my wife
The great news

Go to Jamaica
Cruise to the Bahamas
My wife in a bikini
One hot momma

Select a room
Close to the top
Too close to surface
Stomach in flip-flops

Need to pack light
One piece per person
A five-day cruise
A great excursion

Need my ID
Passport is best
Need piece of mind
No time to rest

Buy new clothes
A pair of sunglasses
A comfortable hat
No free passes

Plan our itinerary
Arriving at port
Stay close to wife
No escort

While on ship
Plenty to eat
Shows to watch
A captain to meet

Drinks and the sun
A dip in the pool
Don't drink too much
Don't be a fool

Activities and games
A little romance
Wine while dining
Time for a dance

Make great memories
Fun in the sun
Get completely rested
Hope you had fun

Morning Routine

Turn off my alarm
Put on coffee to brew
Cream and sugar, or black
It's up to you

Make my bed
Jump in the shower
Pour my first cup of coffee
Grab a bagel to devour

Turn on my laptop
Read the news
Look at my checking account
Nothing new used

Grab my second cup
Clean out the pot
Leave off the burner
It's still too hot

Brush my teeth
Shave my face
Pick out my wardrobe
Tidy up my place

No softball today
So out for my walk
Breathe the fresh air
Wow, no one to talk

Arrive back home
Time for push-ups
Arm curls are next
Now on to sit-ups

Time for yoga
Stretch legs and back
Now comes Tai Chi
There's no time to slack

This sounds exhausting
A lot to take in
I check my calendar
I use a black pen

My routine is over
Time for some tunes
Routines are necessary
Nothing to ruin

Morning Walk

Drink my coffee
Read the news
Finish my bagel
Put on my shoes

Out the door
Down the stairs
No sunglasses needed
There is no glare

Do a little stretching
Loosen up the legs
The body starts to sweat
The body starts to beg

Walking is great exercise
Walking relaxes the mind
Walking with a purpose
Will leave your problems behind

I set a good pace
To increase my heart
I focus my mind
To do my part

And as I walk
I say hi to others
I breathe in fresh air
As not to be smothered

I will walk three miles
That is the goal
Walking is great exercise
Being healthy is gold

Retirement

Entering our golden years
Wanting to be healthy
Looking at our savings
Asking are we wealthy

Having tons of dreams
Travel and vacation
Staying close to family
Or looking at relocation

Time to relax
Enjoy our new life
Wine and reservations
For me and my wife

Fantasies are vivid
Dreams may become real
Our new life
Is now a big deal

We will go on cruises
Soak up the sun
Cocktails in the afternoon
Just having some fun

Maybe we go camping
Visit national parks
Amazed by nature
Redevelop some sparks

Ralph Buelow • 97

Do we have the time
Do we have the money
I have the ambition
Better talk to my honey

I pray we stay safe
I ask we not get ill
I promised myself
To live and chill

I have waited for years
For this day to come
Retiring from work
Marching to a different drum

Senior Softball

Sixty-two is the age you can play
A bat and a glove, it's what you need
Fill out your app
And do your good deed

Twelve is a team
But we need a couple more
Injuries and absences
Will even the score

The count is one and one
As I step into the box
Be patient and selective
And smart like a fox

I hit a fly ball
High in the air
It's drifting towards the line
I hope it stays fair

I'm running the bases
As fast as I can
Now rounding third
The wind blowing me like a fan

I cross home plate
And the team all cheers
The coach shakes my hand
And says, "I'll buy you a beer"

We play nine innings
Just like the pros
The game wears me out
I know I am getting old

After the game
We remove all our gear
We're banged and we're bruised
That's how we play, year after year

The boys of summer
Are the men in the fall
The fountain of youth
Has indeed touched us all

Staying Healthy

Staying healthy
For a retired man
How does one do it
You need a plan

You need to stay disciplined
Stay the course
Eating healthy food
Not eating like a horse

Have a routine
For muscle to gain
Not too strenuous
To cause much pain

One hundred push-ups
Three times a week
The muscles will work
The muscles will tweak

Two hundred sit-ups
Done everyday
Stretching and yoga
Will pave the way

Avoid junk foods
Stay away from the sweets
Protein bars and shakes
Are much better treats

Stay very active
Keep off the couch
Keep the body lean
No stomach or pouch

Get outdoors
Breathe fresh air
Keep the heart healthy
No lives to spare

Recreation

Bonfire

Gather some wood
Stack the logs
Let's all gather round
Me, by my dog

On the beach
At a farm
In the countryside
Let's do no harm

A magical moment
The bonfire blazing
With all my friends
It's truly amazing

Grab the hot dogs
Drink some pop
I've had two dogs
I better stop

Where're the marshmallows
Chocolates and more
Time for dessert
Time for s'mores

Grab my guitar
Play some songs
Please all join in
And sing along

The bonfire burning
Now becoming embers
Gaze at stars
Pictures to remember

Huddle up
Tell some stories
A wonderful night
Take your glory

The bonfire now ashes
Time to put out
Stick and water
Directions I shout

Party is over
Time to turn in
The dawn is approaching
A new day begins

Bowling

Recreational or league
A game with ten pins
Bowling for fun
Or bowling to win

Right or left hand
You decide
Lane's sixty feet long
Not very wide

Plastic or rubber
Conventional or fingertip
Hold the ball firmly
Need a good grip

Start from eight-foot
Or twelve-foot line
Which is comfortable
Which is fine

Do I throw straight
Do I make it curve
No bowling etiquette
Gets on my nerves

I buried the headpin
Left with a split
Where do I stand
Which pin to hit

I threw a strike
I threw a spare
I threw a nine count
Give that pin a glare

Bumpers for kids
Helping them score
Children are happy
Enjoy bowling more

A family event
A night with the guys
A great pastime
Time sure flies

Cars

A car is a frame
Seats and four wheels
Drop in an engine
Now it's a big deal

Some cars were made to race
Some were made for pleasure
Other cars made for luxury
Your car is your treasure

Man will keep his car clean
Maybe give it a name
A car may bring you glory
A car may bring you fame

Critics will say
The future is bright
Cars running on electricity
Some cars in flight

From the Model A and T
To the muscle cars of today
The auto industry is growing
Cars are here to stay

Fishing

One must be patient
In order to fish
Once they are cleaned
It makes a great dish

Do I fish from the bank
Do I fish from a boat
I know I can't swim
This boat better float

Do I dig for worms
Or buy from a store
Do I use artificial
I have lures galore

Do I fish from the bottom
Do I fish with a bobber
Catching certain fish
Requires their heads to be clobbered

A bobber for pan fish
A lure for game
Landing a big trout
Could bring me fame

Fly-fishing for trout
Casting for bass
These fish break surface
Need to reel in fast

Pan fish are scaled
Some, remove skin
A stringer of fish
Is definitely a win

Drop them in breading
Drop them in batter
Having hot oil
Really does matter

As you eat your catch
Be careful of bones
Choking is likely
No life to loan

Half Marathon

From start to finish
Thirteen point one miles long
One needs to train
One must be strong

You need to train
Nineteen-week routine
Strengthen the mind
Make yourself lean

Work on your pulse
Make it low and strong
This race is endurance
Show you belong

Learn how to breathe
Slow, deep breaths
Show the field
You are a threat

There is water
Every other mile
Miss a couple stops
Just run and smile

Others will wonder
What you are doing
Protein candy in my mouth
Energy is what I'm brewing

The race is long
Get a rhythm in mind
Run a strong pace
Leave the rest behind

A quarter mile left
Still feel the groove
No time to let up
Now make your move

Kick into high gear
And earn your place
Your goal's in sight
Win this race

Hunting

My first shotgun
Was a single shot 410
Pheasants are hard to differ
Roosters from hen

My brother and I
Received identical guns
Hunting is serious
But can be fun

We learned how to shoot
By aiming at cans
I enjoy hunting
Now a huge fan

We hunted squirrels
My brother and Dad
Dad never took the first shot
My brother and I were glad

We progressed to pheasant
Quail and rabbit
Hunting is soon
Becoming a habit

I bought a new shotgun
A twelve-gauge pump
Shooting that big gun
Gave my shoulder a thump

What we shot
We intended to eat
Nature is beautiful
And nothing to cheat

Pheasant's flushing
Really startled me bad
The limit was three
I seldom had

My biggest rush
Was tagging a deer
Being shot by others
Was my biggest fear

I wore lots of orange
Head to toe
I used a slug barrel
Instead of a bow

I hunted with cousins
I hunted with friends
We would hunt all day
The sun made us end

I hunted the most
With my high school friend
We still share stories
And will till the end

One must be careful
Look and stay sharp
One wrong mistake
Means angels and harps

Lottery Ticket

I buy my ticket
Twice a week
What're my numbers
I need to peek

Always do a quick pick
Never had much luck
Another losing ticket
I'm beginning to suck

I would share with family
The church and charity
My winnings would spread
To cover with parity

I dream as I sleep
The jackpot is growing
The anticipation of winning
Keeps me going

Spreading the news of winning
Would put shock on their faces
I need a great travel agent
I have a big list of places

I hope someday
It's my turn to win
Big dreams for my family
New lives to begin

Mighty Oak Tree

Home for sparrows and robins
They build their nests
And lay their eggs
A warm, safe place to rest

During the summer
The sun is hot
Rest under its branches
In a cool, shady spot

Grab a tire
Make a swing
Have some laughs
Do your thing

Gather some lumber
Hammer and nails
Make a tree house
Enjoy lunch in a pail

Fall is coming
Leaves are changing colors
Raking leaves into piles
Work, for me and my brother

Acorns are falling to the ground
Squirrels are gathering for food
Winter is fast approaching
Better get in the mood

Oak is hard wood
Burning in your fireplace
Stack it by the cord
Stack it on a sound base

Great for making furniture
Dressers, tables, and chairs
Natural hardwood and color
Furniture with a flair

Pets

Pets are companions
There are many types
Pets are loving
So is the hype

Hamster or guinea pig
Dog or cat
They reduce stress
I like that

A fish in a tank
A housebroken pig
Pets have variety
What do you dig?

Pets for the elderly
Pets for the sick
Dogs are great healers
Your faces they lick

Pets have many uses
That is for sure
They relieve loneliness
What a great cure

Pets in the yard
Pets in the house
Cats are useful
Finding a mouse

Pets need attention
Don't forget the vet
Love at first sight
Once you have met

Scuba Diving

Spending a morning
In a pool
A lot to learn
The instructor was cool

Health questions asked
Concerning the heart
Dying while diving
Not a great start

We learned how to breathe
And come up slow
Rising to the top
Was the goal

Equipment was heavy
And so was the belt
Sixteen pounds on the waist
Was the way to melt

Now time to dive
Show what we learned
A mile in the sun
A sure way to burn

We had air for one hour
Diving fifty feet
Life below the surface
Is awfully sweet

The coral is beautiful
And full of color
I saw a sea turtle
Where was his brother

The fish are fast
Sea life is bright
The sun shining through the water
Was enough light

After one hour
Time to surface
Where was our boat
What was the purpose

We had to swim back
One mile in full gear
My body was tired
No time for tears

I will never forget
The life I saw
The ocean is beautiful
Sea life and all

Ukulele

Originated in Hawaii
This four-string guitar
Play a little tune
Smoke a cigar

Well loved by the royals
Means jumping flea
This little guitar
Are you kidding me

Original strings
Made of animal guts
Hawaiian tunes
In front of my hut

A lot of shapes and sizes
Tenor, concert, bass
Soprano and baritone
What's in your place

Promoted by celebrities
Elvis and Tiny Tim
Beatles and Taylor Swift
This is no whim

Played by Neil Armstrong
After his walk on the moon
Twenty-one days in quarantine
Feeling the gloom

After World War II
Big in Japan
Pop and rock songs
Are you a big fan

"Tiptoe Through the Tulips"
Queen Lili'uokalani's "Aloha 'Oe"
Tuned so much differently
Why is this so

Made by Martin
Sells very cheap
The sound is amazing
Rich and deep

Outdoors

Iowa Winter

The winter is long
The winter is cold
October through April
So I've been told

It can snow anytime
During this span
Need to wear gloves
Or freeze your hand

A snowy countryside
Is beautiful to see
A pretty white blanket
As big as the sea

The snow can be powdery
Or cold and wet
How much can fall
Is anyone's bet

I have seen snowfalls
By the feet
School gets cancelled
This is sweet

Time to make snow forts
Ride your sled
Build a snowman
Cuddle up in bed

I love to ice skate
Play hockey all day
Find a huge hill
To ride my sleigh

At the end of the day
Hot cocoa to drink
Remove all your layers
Warm skin back to pink

Snow is hard work
Driveway to clear
In blizzard conditions
Requires my winter gear

Riding through the countryside
A sleigh pulled by a horse
The scenery is spectacular
It's magical, of course

Winter is long
Winter is fun
But I love summer
And the hot Iowa sun

Iowa

Iowa is known
As the Hawkeye State
Bordered by two rivers
A Midwest estate?

Has the world's largest truck stop
Iowa 80 is the name
Birthplace of Bob Feller
Home of John Wayne

More hogs than humans
Over 85,000 farms
Iowans are Christians
Meaning no harm

We produce soybeans and cereal
Number one producer of corn
The agricultural center
Iowa, toot you horn

Home of the largest wooden nickel
And *Field of Dreams*
Inventing sliced bread
Makes Iowans beam

Birthplace of our thirty-first leader
Three states in one city
Iowans working the land
While showing no pity

Des Moines is the capital
Replacing Iowa City
Founder of the electronic digital computer
Making us witty

Iowa is the only state
That begins with two vowels
Home of the Red Delicious apple
Iowa deserves a bow

Iowa took Buddy Holly
Ritchie Valens and crew
Crashed near Clear Lake
The world soon knew

Hosting the RAGBRAI
The oldest bike-touring event
First moving-train robbery
History was meant

One city island
They call Sabula
The Shrine of the Grotto of
the Redemption
Portraying the life of Jesus, hallelujah

Home of the Largest Bullhead statue
And largest strawberry lives here
Twenty-five percent of power generated
by wind
All in Iowa, how weird

Iowa has seventy-five facts
Too many to list
Iowa is amazing
You get the gist

Mississippi River

Second-largest river in North America
Running through ten states
Providing power to cities
With dams and their gates

The Mother Fauna of North America
Over 2,300 miles long
Flooding every spring
Back in your banks where you belong

The Great River Road
Runs alongside the river
Commerce is important
The barges they deliver

The fourth-largest river in the world
Over two hundred feet deep
The river can kill
Families will weep

The river is home
To 25 percent of all fish species
A fascinating fact
A wonderful thesis

Seasons

The song says
The seasons have all gone
The seasons remain
Singing poetic songs

The seasons change
As the earth rotates
New life begins
It's worth the wait

When spring arrives
The flowers bloom
Such beautiful colors
No more winter gloom

The rains commence
Nature speaks out
Hibernation is over
There is no doubt

Along comes summer
The sun heats up
Parks and picnics
Bring paper cups

Swimming in pools
Boating on the river
Skiing and tubing
Save me a sliver

Summer fades away
Fall settles in
Trees change colors
School begins

Farmers are harvesting
Hunters in their stands
Firewood being chopped
I need a lending hand

High school football
Homecoming dances
Camping and bonfires
Leads to romances

A couple of snow flurries
Halloween is done
Winter is approaching
Gone is the sun

The winter seems long
The temperature is cold
Fireplaces are crackling
Stories are told

Snowmen are made
Ice skating and sledding
Nature hunkers down
Animals done shedding

Four seasons in one year
Three hundred sixty-five days in all
Nature will warn you
Nature will call

Tornado

A force of nature
Devastating destruction
Insurance adjusters
Means new construction

From Texas to Kansas
Known as Tornado Alley
A deadly path
Rising fatality

Massive wind speeds
Up to 300 miles per hour
Tornadoes will kill
Tornadoes will devour

For a couple of minutes
Usually on ground
Seventy-five feet high
Makes a loud sound

Measured by a scale
F0 to F5
Traveling up to fifty miles
This is no jive

Known as cyclones
Or even as twisters
Head to your cellar
Take your sister

Even on water
Known as a waterspout
Land or water
Leave no doubt

A deadly storm
That has no season
Predicting its path
Has no reason

Life Advice

Advice

Fight the wars
You know you can win
Don't engage the battle
No need to begin

This doesn't mean
To duke it out
Life has more obstacles
Life has more bouts

Nor are we fighting
With other foes
Life is more precious
Still a long way to go

This may be a conflict
With a friend or boss
Forgo the arguing
Just take the loss

A simple misunderstanding
At home with your wife
Relationship's not worth wrecking
Better opportunities in life

It's not about right
Nor about who's wrong
Life is already tough enough
Just learn how to get along

It's about learning to listen
How to agree
Find common ground
This is how to succeed

Have your ducks in a row
Proceed with a plan
Learn how to rebut
Learn how to land

It's okay to disagree
Find a solution
Both sides involved
Make new resolutions

Christmas Cookies

From generation to generation
Over the holiday season
Baking Christmas cookies
What a great reason

Find Grandma's recipes
Pick out the right one
My mother taught me
Precious time won

Out in the kitchen
Pick out the cookie
Father and son
Son is a rookie

Reading a recipe
Is no big trick
Mixer and bowl
Gives us something to lick

Roll out the dough
With a wooden rolling pin
Cutting out cookies
Makes my son grin

Place on a cookie sheet
Get ready to bake
Set the timer
More cookies we make

The cookies are done
Pull out the sheet
The cookies look great
Hot cookies we eat

Let the cookies cool down
Clean up our mess
My son, the chef
Now needs to rest

Tradition is important
Please pass them on
Family can enjoy
Long after we're gone

COVID-19

Originating in China
Coming from a bat
Some are arguing
Tit for tat

Vaccines were discovered
Arriving at warp speed
Mandates were warranted
Republicans saying no need

Democrats will argue
Get the shot
The Red will argue
Tempers are hot

Republicans say
There is no need
It is our choice
Pleading natural immunity

One thing is for certain
COVID spreads fast
Avoid the infection
Vaccination will last

COVID is mutating
Pandemic will spread
You have two choices
Live or be dead

Death

Ashes to ashes
Dust to dust
If God doesn't want you
The devil must

A poem I learned
As a child
The words are powerful
The meaning is wild

Will I see angels
A white, pearly gate
Will I see a bright light
I can wait

Have you asked for forgiveness
Are you at peace
Are you ready for God
To have your soul released

Do I get buried
Six feet in the ground
Family is hurting
Pity is found

Do I get cremated
Ashes in urn
Catholics say no
Meaning no burn

What is my legacy
A miserable old man
A loving father
What's God's plan

I took my last breath
Forever to sleep
No family present
No one to weep

Life is eternal
Is my belief
I suffer no more
Please feel relief

Close your eyes
Envision my face
I live in your heart
A loving place

Jesus

Who is this
What is He
Dying on the cross
Is not for me

Born in a manger
A baby like you and me
King Herod is coming
Joseph and Mary must flee

Life was normal
Preaching the good news
Living in Jerusalem
Born to be a Jew

Drawing vast crowds
With miracles and more
Healing the sick
Feeding the poor

Baptized by John
In the Jordan River
Casting out all sins
Our souls He delivers

We are made
In the image of God
Jesus is my Savior
To God I nod

It is written
That we are children of God
A powerful army
An almighty pod

He had twelve men
To follow Him
They were the foundation
Jesus was the gem

Captured by Pilate
To die on the cross
Life everlasting
Now is not loss

Buried in a tomb
Jesus rose on the third day
Jesus Christ our Savior
To Jesus I pray

Reflections

Christmas is coming; it's almost here
Time for presents and holiday cheer
They say 'tis the season
I see hatred, protests,
and plain old treason
Where is the love
Do we really need a reason

Ah, the magic of Christmas,
what powerful words
The crackling of logs, the singing of birds
But what does it mean? Does it
come from the heart?
Is it power and money? I think
we are miles apart

Politicians say take Christ out of Christmas
For it offends
I promise you one thing
Christ will be there waiting at the end

The spirit of Saint Nick
Should be more than a month
Family and love are not tricks
Open your hearts and
welcome God's family

Be kind and generous
What a wonderful homily
They say wisdom comes with age
Sinning and arguing is at what stage

Forgive and be strong
Life can be short, or beautiful and long
I have learned to be quiet and listen
My ears are happy and my heart glistens

Enjoy the season
Laugh and be merry
Family is waiting
What a wonderful reason

Tennis Shoes

Made for tennis
Made for running
Stylish and comfortable
Really quite stunning

Made for baseball
Made for walking
Made for basketball
Keep on talking

Everyday life
Labeled casual wear
Made now in leather
Canvas would tear

High-tops or oxford
Very practical uses
Made for everyone
Leaves no excuses

Endorsed by athletes
The biggest stars
Worn with suits
Pocketing cigars

Wear them with socks
Wear them barefoot
May cause blisters and bleeding
This is well put

I love my tennis shoes
I wear them every day
I wear them for work
I wear them for play

The Golden Rule

Do unto others as you would
Have them do unto you
A powerful phrase
From the old school

What does it mean
How to apply
Many people feel
Turn a blind eye

The Bible says
"Love thy neighbor"
Cease the hatred
Do us a favor

Think of a world
With no more war
No more bloodshed
Just an even score

Think of a world
With brothers and sisters
No more friction
No more blisters

Political leaders
Take a hard, long look
Rid the world
Of all these crooks

Think of a place
With one common goal
Love all mankind
Heal the soul

The Good Old Days

A well-used phrase
Meaning the past
A youthful time
Life was a blast

How old were the days
How long did they stay
Getting ahead meant
We're making hay

Life was simple
Technology not born
Most were innocent
Lives not torn

Kickball in the street
Tag with your friends
Biking and laughing
No fighting to mend

Parents and neighbors
Sitting on their porch
Differences discussed
Businesses not torched

Iced tea was common
As was lemonade
Entertainment was cheap
Cards being played

Television was basic
Three channels to choose
Great family time
Nothing to lose

Records were played
No CDs or tapes
Reading comic books
Wearing Superman capes

Please and thank you
Manners were stressed
Church on Sunday
Going well dressed

Full-service gas stations
To take care of cars
One in most neighborhoods
Not traveling far

Drive-in theaters
A Saturday matinee
Movies rated G
Meaning safe to play

Roller-skating rinks
Parks for kids
Zoos for families
Were all we did

Technology now born
The world is shrinking
Automation driven
People not thinking

The Rose

Are you feeling down
Feeling the blues
A rose may say
I love you

There are over 300 species
And that's divine
It's mentioned in the Bible
And can also mean wine

A rose symbolizes Mary
Purity, sorrow, and glory
A rose has a meaning
And surely tells a story

Pink means grace or joy
Red stands for love
White is purity or innocence
From the heavens above

Yellow is for friendship
Orange is passion or gratitude
A rose has many meanings
Truly has an attitude

Only one of three flowers
Mentioned in the Bible
A rose may be a lifesaver
And most certainly reliable

Given by the dozen
Or as a single bloom
It changes your mood
Wipes away the gloom

Such a beautiful flower
Yet it has thorns
One must admire its beauty
The rose is adorned

CPSIA information can be obtained
at www.ICGtesting.com
Printed in the USA
BVHW090859050522
635996BV00062B/4320